Patterns of Change

TABLES AND GRAPHS

T E R C

Investigations in Number, Data, and Space®

Dale Seymour Publications®

Menlo Park, California

The *Investigations* curriculum was developed at TERC (formerly Technical Education Research Centers) in collaboration with Kent State University and the State University of New York at Buffalo. The work was supported in part by National Science Foundation Grant No. ESI-9050210. TERC is a nonprofit company working to improve mathematics and science education. TERC is located at 2067 Massachusetts Avenue, Cambridge, MA 02140.

This project was supported, in part,
by the
National Science Foundation
Opinions expressed are those of the authors
and not necessarily those of the Foundation

Managing Editor: Catherine Anderson
Series Editor: Beverly Cory
Manuscript Editor: Karen Becker
ESL Consultant: Nancy Sokol Green
Production/Manufacturing Director: Janet Yearian
Production/Manufacturing Coordinator: Joe Conte
Design Manager: Jeff Kelly
Design: Don Taka
Illustrations: Susan Jaekel, Carl Yoshihara
Composition: Archetype Book Composition

This book is published by Dale Seymour Publications®, an imprint of Addison Wesley Longman, Inc.

Dale Seymour Publications
2725 Sand Hill Road
Menlo Park, CA 94025
Customer Service: 800-872-1100

DALE
SEYMOUR
PUBLICATIONS®

Order number DS47058
ISBN 1-57232-811-8
1 2 3 4 5 6 7 8 9 10-ML-01 00 99 98 97

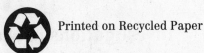
Printed on Recycled Paper

Contents

*Repeated-use sheet

ONE-CENTIMETER GRAPH PAPER

1

Tile Pattern Template

Growing Tile Pattern

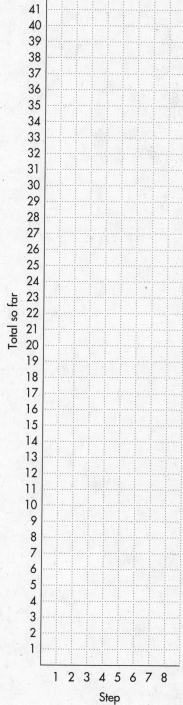

Step number	New tiles (step size)	Total so far
1		
2		
3		
4		
5		
6		
7		
8		

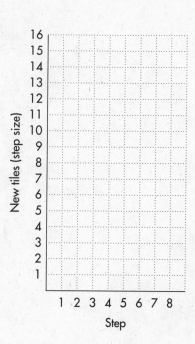

Tile Pattern Template

Growing Tile Pattern

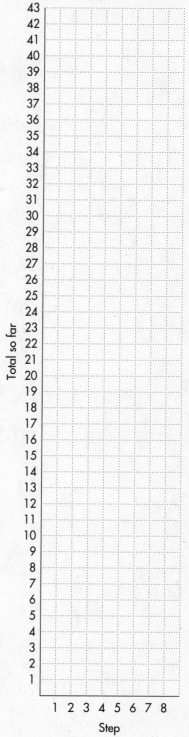

Step number	New tiles (step size)	Total so far
1		
2		
3		
4		
5		
6		
7		
8		

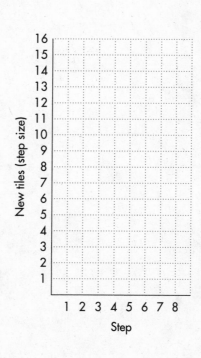

Growing Tile Patterns

Draw a pattern that changes in some regular way. You can color the pattern if you wish. Then fill in the table to show the step size and the total number of tiles in the pattern after each step.

Step number	New tiles (step size)	Total so far
1		
2		
3		
4		
5		
6		
7		
8		

Finally, describe generally how your tile pattern grows:

_____

_____

_____

To the Family

Growing Tile Patterns

Sessions 1–2

Math Content
Building and describing patterns that change in a regular way

Materials
Student Sheet 2
Pencil
Colored pencils, crayons, or markers (optional)

In class, we have been exploring tile patterns and analyzing how they "grow." For homework, your child will draw a new pattern that changes in a regular way on the grid on Student Sheet 2. Each square in the grid represents a "tile." Your child will then fill in the table by showing the *step size* (how many new "tiles," or grid squares, were added to the pattern at each new step) and the total number of tiles (squares) in the pattern after each step. Finally, your child will describe generally how the tile pattern grows (for example, "It keeps getting bigger, but it alternates between steps of 2 and steps of 4.").

Growing and Graphing Tile Patterns

Draw one tile pattern, and fill in the table and graphs. You may use any of the tile patterns we discussed in class or one of your own.

Step number	New tiles (step size)	Total so far
1		
2		
3		
4		
5		
6		
7		
8		

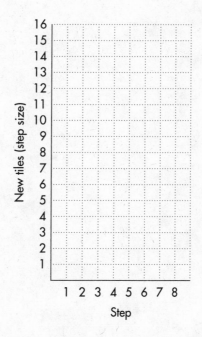

To the Family

Growing and Graphing Tile Patterns

Sessions 1–2

Math Content
Making tables and graphs that describe growing tile patterns

Materials
Student Sheet 3
Pencil
Colored pencils, crayons, or markers (optional)

In class, we have continued to explore growing patterns made of tiles, and tables and graphs that go with those patterns. For homework, your child will draw another pattern that changes in a regular way and fill in the table on Student Sheet 3. Your child will then fill in the graphs to represent the data in the table. The smaller graph will show the step size changes (from column 2), and the larger graph will show the total number of tiles in the pattern (from column 3).

Growing Tile Patterns (page 1 of 4)

Twos Tower

Start

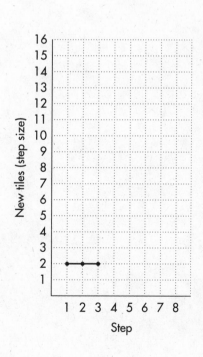

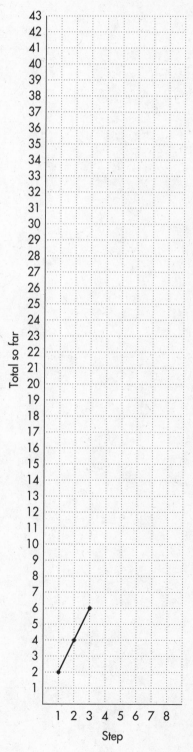

Step number	New tiles (step size)	Total so far
1	2	2
2	2	4
3	2	6
4	2	
5	2	
6		
7		
8		

Growing Tile Patterns (page 2 of 4)

Squares

Start

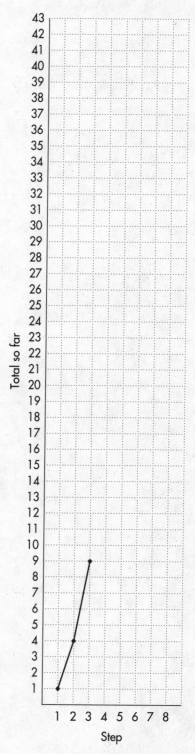

Total so far

Step number	New tiles (step size)	Total so far
1	1	1
2	3	4
3	5	9
4		
5		
6		
7		
8		
0		

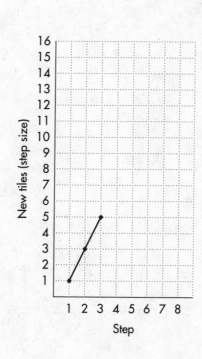

Name _____ Date _____

Growing Tile Patterns (page 3 of 4)

Staircase

Start

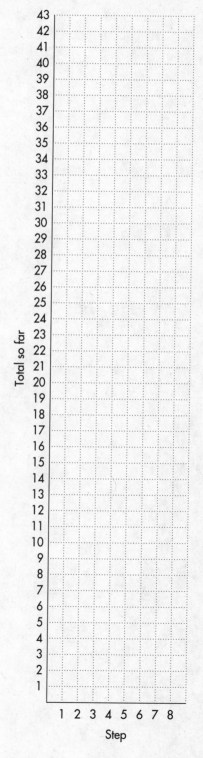

Step number	New tiles (step size)	Total so far
1	1	1
2	2	3
3	3	6
4		
5		
6		
7		
8		

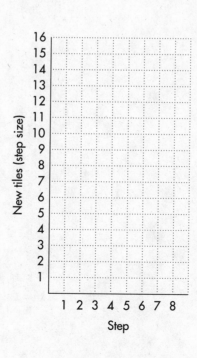

Growing Tile Patterns (page 4 of 4)

Doubling

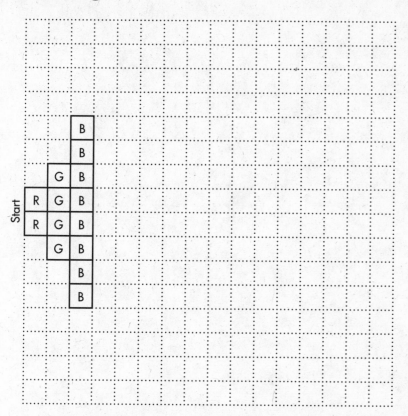

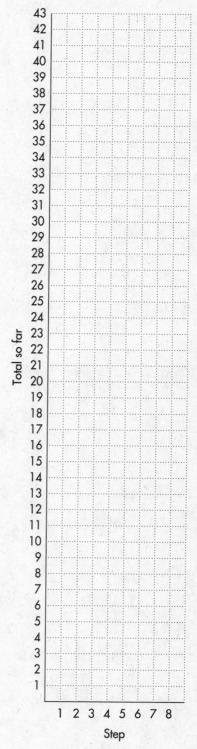

Step number	New tiles (step size)	Total so far
1	2	2
2	4	6
3	8	14
4	16	30
5		
6		
7		
8		

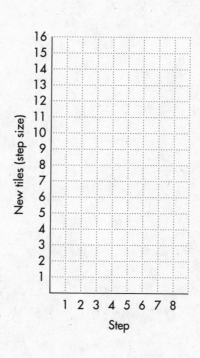

Same Numbers, Different Pattern

Choose a pattern from Student Sheet 4. Draw different growing patterns that fit the numbers in the table for the pattern you chose.

I chose: Twos Tower   Squares   Staircase   Doubling

Describe how your tile pattern grows:

_____

_____

_____

_____

Be sure to bring all of Student Sheet 4 back to class for discussion in the next math class.

To the Family

Same Numbers, Different Pattern

Sessions 3–4

Math Content
Making several growing designs to fit the same table of numbers

Materials
Student Sheet 4
Student Sheet 5
Colored pencils, crayons, or markers
Pencil

In class, we have been exploring how different growing designs can fit the same table of numbers. For homework, your child will choose one of the tables on Student Sheet 4. On Student Sheet 5, he or she will draw several growing designs that can fit the numbers in the table. Your child may want to use some of the tile patterns that were developed in class for patterns posters. Remind your child to take all of Student Sheet 4 back to class for discussion during the next math class.

Describing a Straight Line Trip

1. Plan a trip along a straight line. Be sure your trip has some changes of speed. Invent a way to show the changing speeds on paper *without words* and *without a key*. You may make a table if you wish.

2. Ask someone at home to act out your trip. Make any changes to your representation that are necessary to make the trip easier for the person to understand and interpret. Ask the person to try again and continue making changes until the person can act out the trip correctly.

3. Write about what the person did and didn't understand, and describe any changes you made to your representation in order to make it clearer.

_____

_____

_____

_____

_____

_____

To the Family

Describing a Straight Line Trip

Session 1

Math Content
Developing informal representations for speed, time, and distance

Materials
Student Sheet 6
Pencil

In class, students have been planning and acting out trips of varying speeds along a straight line, and developing ways to make representations on paper of those trips. For homework, your child will plan a short walking trip of varying speeds along any straight line on the floor, and will then invent his or her own way of showing the changing speeds on paper, without using words and without a key. Your child will ask someone at home to use the representation to describe and act out the trip. Your child will then write about what the person did and didn't understand, and describe any changes made to the representation to make it easier to understand and interpret.

Template for Tables

Time

Time (seconds)	Total distance so far (meters)
2	
4	
6	
8	
10	
12	
14	

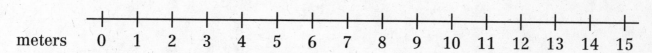

meters 0 1 2 3 4 5 6 7 8 9 10 11 12 13 14 15

Time (seconds)	Total distance so far (meters)
2	
4	
6	
8	
10	
12	
14	

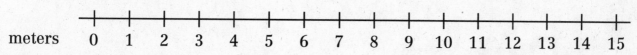

meters 0 1 2 3 4 5 6 7 8 9 10 11 12 13 14 15

Height of a Girl

This table lists the heights of a girl from age 7 to 17.

Make a graph of her changing height.

Age (years)	Height (inches)	Growth in last year
7	48	
8	50	
9	52	
10	54	
11	56	
12	59	
13	62	
14	65	
15	66	
16	67	
17	67	

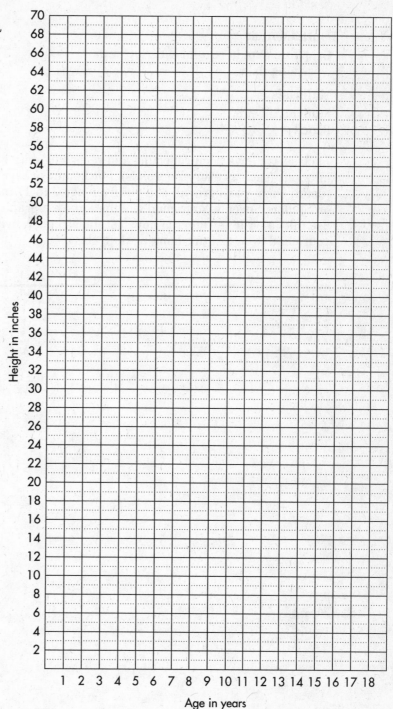

Tell the story of the girl's growth. When did she grow fast? When did she grow slowly? What is happening to her growth at the end?

27

To the Family

Height of a Girl

Session 2

Math Content
Graphing data in regular time intervals
Analyzing data

Materials
Student Sheet 8
Pencil

In class, we have been collecting and recording data in regular time intervals (such as every 2 seconds). For homework, your child will record each year's growth of a girl from age 7 to 17 in the third column on Student Sheet 8. Your child will then make a graph of the data and use this to write the story of how fast the girl grew over time. Remind your child to return this homework to class.

Three Motion Stories

Plan a trip for one of the following stories. Make a
table showing where the person would be every
2 seconds (that is, where the beanbags would land).

Story A   Run a few steps, stop, run a few steps,
stop, then walk to the end.

Story B   Walk very slowly a short way, stop for
about 6 seconds, and then walk fast to
the end.

Story C   Run about halfway, then go slower and
slower until the end.

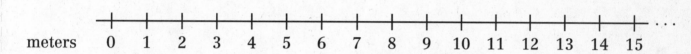

meters   0   1   2   3   4   5   6   7   8   9   10   11   12   13   14   15   · · ·

Time (seconds)	Total distance so far (meters)
2	
4	
6	
8	
10	
12	
14	

Graph of a Trip

Distance (meters)

Time (seconds)

To the Family

Graph of a Trip

Session 3

Math Content
Interpreting a graph of distance over time

Materials
Student Sheet 10
Pencil

In class, we have been matching tables with motion stories. For homework, your child will write the story of a person's imaginary "trip" along a straight line. The graph of the "trip" is shown on Student Sheet 10. Your child will tell how the person was moving for each part—fast, slow, or not at all—by writing notes directly on the graph or elsewhere on the student sheet. Your child might make a table from the graph in order to help interpret the information. We will share the interpretations of this graph at the beginning of the next math class.

Graph Template

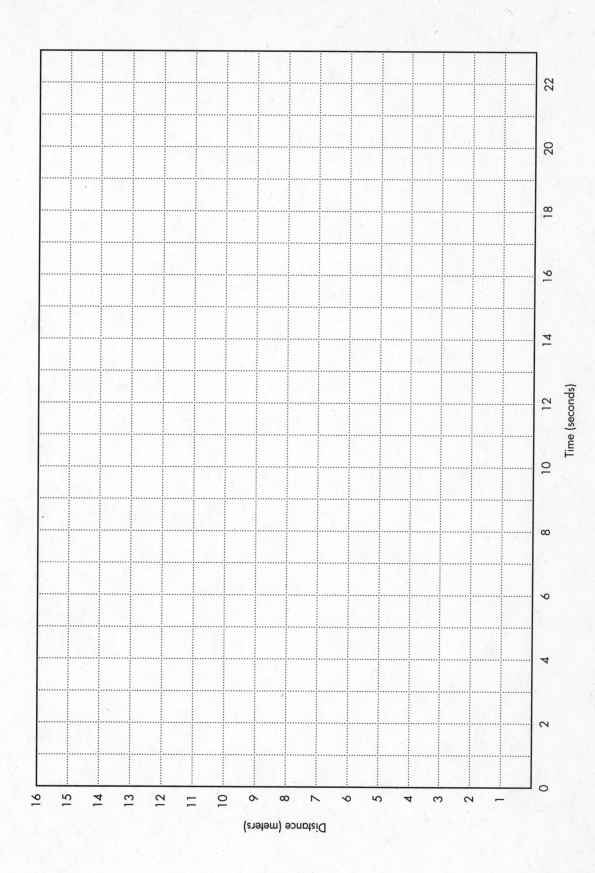

Distance (meters)

16
15
14
13
12
11
10
9
8
7
6
5
4
3
2
1

0   2   4   6   8   10   12   14   16   18   20   22

Time (seconds)

Investigation 2 • Session 4
Patterns of Change

Planning and Graphing a Trip

Plan a story about any sort of trip. It could be a walking or sailing trip, a trip by train or car, or any other idea you may have. Write the story below. Then make a graph to go with it on Student Sheet 13.

Explain how the graph shows the changes of speed that happen in the story. Make the story, graph, and explanation clear enough to be used to teach a fourth grade student how to read the graph. You may want to add a table to make the description of the trip clearer on the back of this sheet.

To the Family

Planning and Graphing a Trip

Session 4

Math Content
Making a line graph of distance versus time

Materials
Student Sheet 12
Student Sheet 13
One-centimeter graph paper (optional)
Pencil

In class, we have been making graphs that show distance over time. For homework, your child will plan a story about any sort of trip. It could be a walking or sailing trip, a trip made by train or car, or any other idea your child might have. After writing the story, your child will make a graph to go with it and explain how the graph shows the changes of speed that happen in the story.

Another Graph Template

Distance (meters)

16
15
14
13
12
11
10
9
8
7
6
5
4
3
2
1

0   2   4   6   8   10   12   14   16   18   20   22

Time (seconds)

To the Family

Planning and Graphing a Trip

Session 4

Math Content
Making a line graph of distance versus time

Materials
Student Sheet 12
Student Sheet 13
One-centimeter graph paper (optional)
Pencil

In class, we have been making graphs that show distance over time. For homework, your child will plan a story about any sort of trip. It could be a walking or sailing trip, a trip made by train or car, or any other idea your child might have. After writing the story, your child will make a graph to go with it and explain how the graph shows the changes of speed that happen in the story.

ONE-CENTIMETER GRAPH PAPER

To the Family

Planning and Graphing a Trip

Session 4

Math Content
Making a line graph of distance versus time

Materials
Student Sheet 12
Student Sheet 13
One-centimeter graph paper (optional)
Pencil

In class, we have been making graphs that show distance over time. For homework, your child will plan a story about any sort of trip. It could be a walking or sailing trip, a trip made by train or car, or any other idea your child might have. After writing the story, your child will make a graph to go with it and explain how the graph shows the changes of speed that happen in the story.

Matching Stories, Tables, and Graphs (page 1 of 2)

Cut apart the stories, the tables, and the graphs.
Which ones match? Group them together.
Finish filling in the tables, and write the missing story.

Story 1 Walk slowly about halfway and then run until the end.

Story 2 Run about halfway, stop for 4 seconds, then walk to the end.

Story 3

Table A

Time (seconds)	Distance in previous 2 seconds (step size)	Total distance (meters)
2	1	1
4	1	2
6	1	3
8		4
10		5
11		8
12		11
14		

Table B

Time (seconds)	Distance in previous 2 seconds (step size)	Total distance (meters)
2	2	2
4	2	4
6	2	6
8		7
10		5
12		3
14		1
16		

Matching Stories, Tables, and Graphs (page 2 of 2)

Table C

Time (seconds)	Distance in previous 2 seconds (step size)	Total distance (meters)
2		
4		
6		
8		
10		
12		
14		

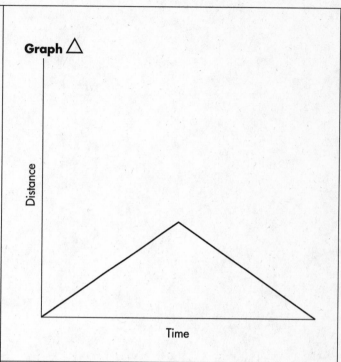

Graph △

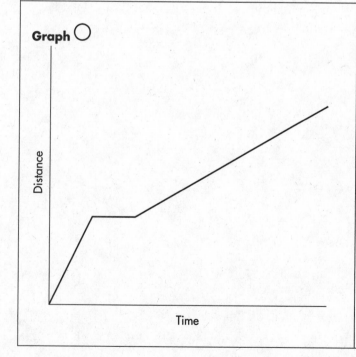

Graph ○

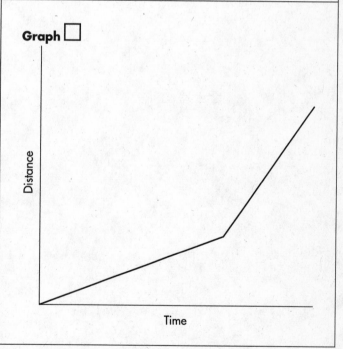

Graph □

Trips Computer Screen

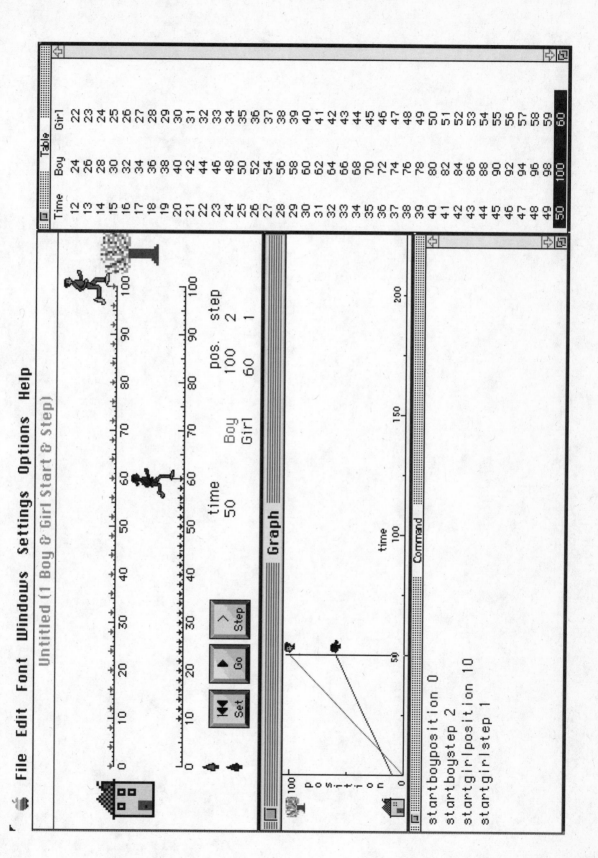

Trips in *Setting* 1 (page 1 of 2)

Create a trip for Motion Stories 1, 2, and 3. Use either the meterstick or the computer. In the blanks, write the values for position and step size that you used for each trip.

Note: If you have done a story with the meterstick, check it on the computer if you have time.

___

Motion Story 1 The girl gets to the tree way ahead of the boy.

startboyposition _____   *(The boy is going to start at position __?__)*

startboystep _____   *(The boy is going to walk with a step size of __?__)*

startgirlposition _____   *(The girl is going to start at position __?__)*

startgirlstep _____   *(The girl is going to walk with a step size of __?__)*

___

Motion Story 2 The girl starts behind the boy, but she passes the boy and gets to the tree first.

startboyposition _____

startboystep _____

startgirlposition _____

startgirlstep _____

___

Motion Story 3 The boy starts at the tree and the girl starts at the house. The boy gets to the house before the girl gets to the tree.

startboyposition _____

startboystep _____

startgirlposition _____

startgirlstep _____

Choose the trip for one story and use it to fill in the next page. Record here which story you choose: _____

Trips in Setting 1 (page 2 of 2)

Tell how the trip would look from
the point of view of either the boy
or the girl.

Time	Position of boy	Position of girl
0		

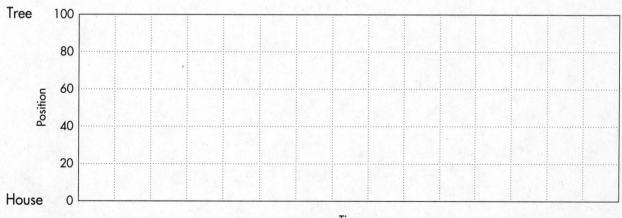

Story of a Trip (page 1 of 2)

Story

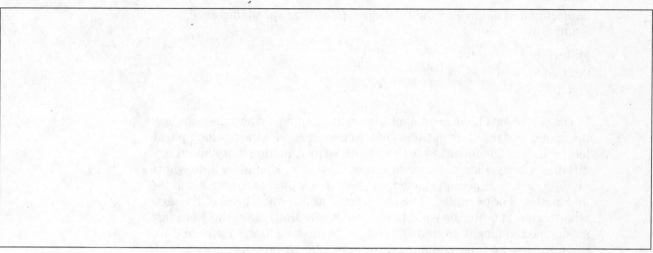

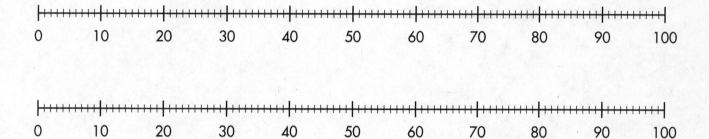

Time (seconds)	Position of boy (meters)		Time (seconds)	Position of girl (meters)

To the Family

Story of a Trip

Session 2

Math Content

Exploring and describing the relationships among speed, distance, and time

Materials

Student Sheet 17
Pencil

In class, students have been exploring what happens when they change the speed and the start positions of two travelers who move along parallel tracks. For homework, your child will write a motion story about a girl and a boy walking along two tracks. The story should include where on the track each person started, the speed at which each went, and the destination. For example, "The boy started at 30, way ahead of the girl, who started at 0. But he went to the tree really slowly and she went fast, so she passed him at around 70, and got to the tree first." Your child will fill in the tracks, tables, and graph to match his or her story.

Story of a Trip (page 2 of 2)

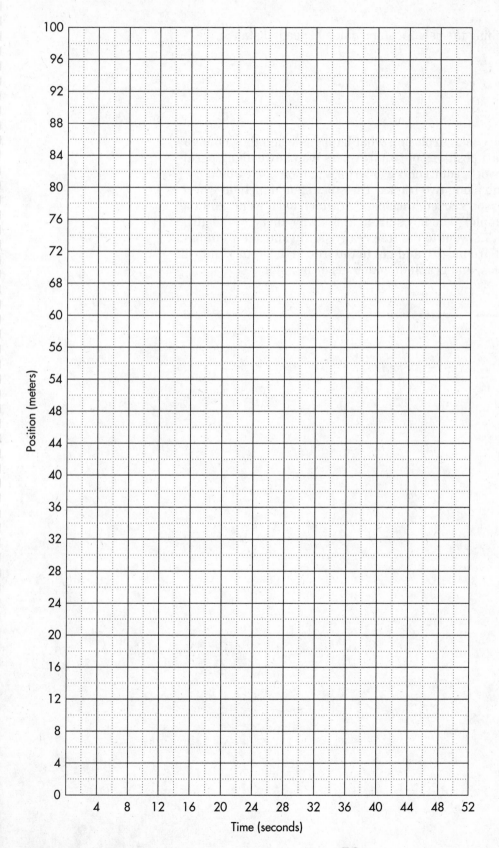

To the Family

Story of a Trip

Session 2

Math Content

Exploring and describing the relationships among speed, distance,
  and time

Materials

Student Sheet 17
Pencil

In class, students have been exploring what happens when they change
the speed and the start positions of two travelers who move along parallel tracks. For homework, your child will write a motion story about a
girl and a boy walking along two tracks. The story should include where
on the track each person started, the speed at which each went, and the
destination. For example, "The boy started at 30, way ahead of the girl,
who started at 0. But he went to the tree really slowly and she went fast,
so she passed him at around 70, and got to the tree first." Your child will
fill in the tracks, tables, and graph to match his or her story.

Using the *Trips* Settings

Setting 1

```
startboyposition 50
startboystep -1
startgirlposition 0
startgirlstep 3
```

	Boy		Girl	
Time	Step size	Position	Step size	Position
0	–1	50	3	0
1	–1	49	3	3
2	–1	48	3	6
3		47		9
4				
5				
6				
7				

Setting 2

```
startboyposition 0
startboystep 2
startgirlposition 0
startgirlstep 4
changeboystepto 8
  [when boyposition = 4]
changegirlstepto 6
  [when girlposition = 12]
```

	Boy		Girl	
Time	Step size	Position	Step size	Position
0	2	0	4	0
1	2	2	4	4
2	2	4	4	8
3	8	12	4	12
4	8	20	6	18
5		28		24
6				
7				

Setting 3

```
startboyposition 0
startboystep 0
startgirlposition 0
startgirlstep 10
changeboystepby 1 [always]
changegirlstepby -1
[always]
```

	Boy		Girl	
Time	Step size	Position	Step size	Position
0	0	0	10	0
1	1	0	9	10
2	2	1	8	19
3	3	3		
4	4	6		
5				
6				
7				

Trips in Setting 2 (page 1 of 2)

Create a trip for Motion Stories 1, 2, and 3. In the blanks,
write the values for position and step size.

Note: If you have done a story with the meterstick, check
it on the computer if you have time.

Motion Story 1 The girl gets to the tree way ahead of the boy.

startboyposition ____   startboystep ____

startgirlposition ____   startgirlstep ____

changeboystepto ____ [when boyposition = ____]

   (The boy changes his step size to ? when he reaches position ?)

changegirlstepto ____ [when girlposition = ____]

   (The girl changes her step size to ? when she reaches position ?)

Motion Story 2 The girl starts behind the boy, but she passes
the boy and gets to the tree first.

startboyposition ____   startboystep ____

startgirlposition ____   startgirlstep ____

changeboystepto ____ [when boyposition = ____]

changegirlstepto ____ [when girlposition = ____]

Motion Story 3 The boy starts at the tree and the girl starts
at the house. The boy gets to the house *before* the girl gets
to the tree.

startboyposition ____   startboystep ____

startgirlposition ____   startgirlstep ____

changeboystepto ____ [when boyposition = ____]

changegirlstepto ____ [when girlposition = ____]

Choose the trip for one story and use it to fill in the next page.
Record here which story you choose: _____

Trips in Setting 2 (page 2 of 2)

Tell how the trip would look from the
point of view of either the boy or the girl.

Time	Position of boy	Position of girl
0		

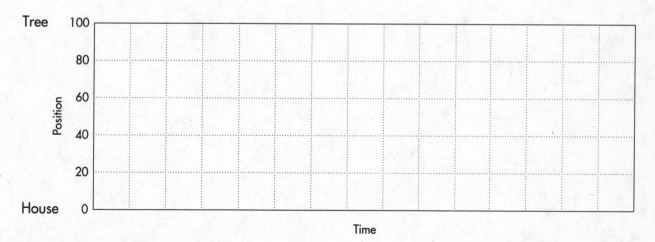

Trips in Setting 3 (page 1 of 2)

Create a trip for Motion Stories 1, 2, and 3. In the blanks, write the values for position and step size.

Motion Story 1 The girl gets to the tree way ahead of the boy.

startboyposition ____   startboystep ____

startgirlposition ____   startgirlstep ____

changeboystepby ____ [always]

   (*At every step, the boy changes his step size by __?__*)

changegirlstepto____ [always]

   (*At every step, the girl changes her step size by __?__*)

Motion Story 2 The girl starts behind the boy, but she passes the boy and gets to the tree first.

startboyposition ____   startboystep ____

startgirlposition ____   startgirlstep ____

changeboystepto ____ [always]

changegirlstepto ____ [always]

Motion Story 3 The boy starts at the tree and the girl starts at the house. The boy gets to the house before the girl gets to the tree.

startboyposition ____   startboystep ____

startgirlposition ____   startgirlstep ____

changeboystepto ____ [always]

changegirlstepto ____ [always]

Choose the trip for one story and use it to fill in the next page. Record here which story you choose: _____

61

Trips in Setting 3 (page 2 of 2)

Tell how the trip would look from the
point of view of either the boy or the girl.

Time	Position of boy	Position of girl
0		

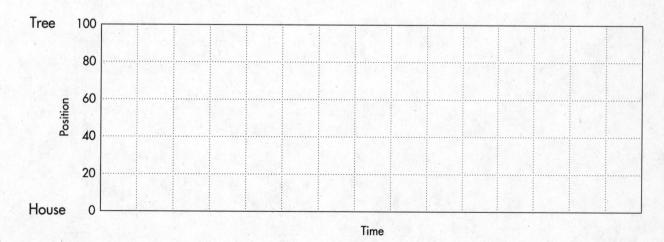

Investigation 3 • Session 3
Patterns of Change

Story of a Trip (page 1 of 2)

Story

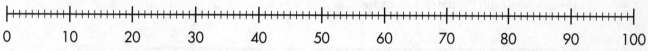

Time (seconds)	Position of boy (meters)		Time (seconds)	Position of girl (meters)

To the Family

Story of a Trip with Varying Step Sizes

Session 3

Math Content

Exploring and describing the relationships among speed, distance
and time

Materials

Student Sheet 17
Pencil

In class, students have continued exploring what happens when they
change the speed and the start positions of two travelers along parallel
tracks. For homework, your child will write another motion story for
a girl and a boy who walk along two tracks. The story should include
where on the track each person started, the speed at which each went,
where and how the trip changed, and the destination. This time the trip
will also involve a *change* in step size. For example, "The boy starts with
a step size of 2 and then changes to a step size of 8 when he reaches the
4 on the track. The girl's step size starts at 4 and changes to 6 when she
reaches the position 12 on the track." Your child will fill in the tracks,
tables, and graph to match her or his story.

Name _____ Date _____

Story of a Trip (page 2 of 2)

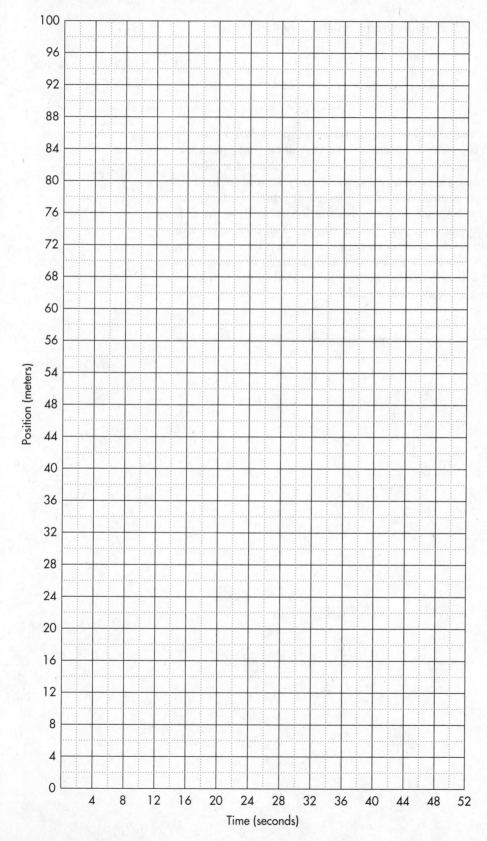

To the Family

Story of a Trip with Varying Step Sizes

Session 3

Math Content

Exploring and describing the relationships among speed, distance
   and time

Materials

Student Sheet 17
Pencil

In class, students have continued exploring what happens when they
change the speed and the start positions of two travelers along parallel
tracks. For homework, your child will write another motion story for
a girl and a boy who walk along two tracks. The story should include
where on the track each person started, the speed at which each went,
where and how the trip changed, and the destination. This time the trip
will also involve a *change* in step size. For example, "The boy starts with
a step size of 2 and then changes to a step size of 8 when he reaches the
4 on the track. The girl's step size starts at 4 and changes to 6 when she
reaches the position 12 on the track." Your child will fill in the tracks,
tables, and graph to match her or his story.

Story of a Trip (page 1 of 2)

Story

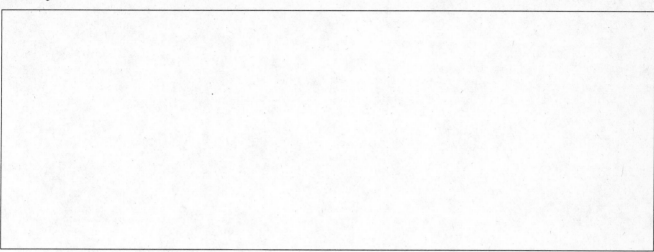

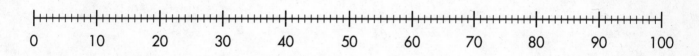

Time (seconds)	Position of boy (meters)		Time (seconds)	Position of girl (meters)

Name _____ Date _____

Story of a Trip (page 2 of 2)

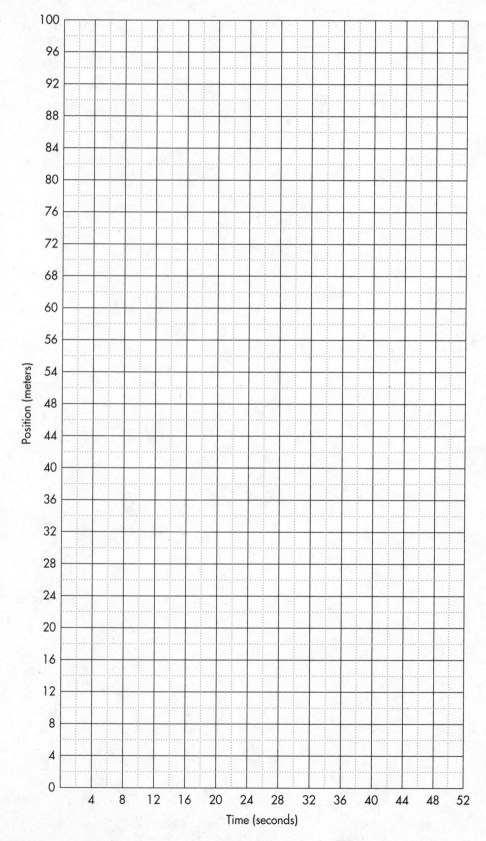

71

Two Kinds of Graphs (page 1 of 2)

Time (seconds)	Position	Step size

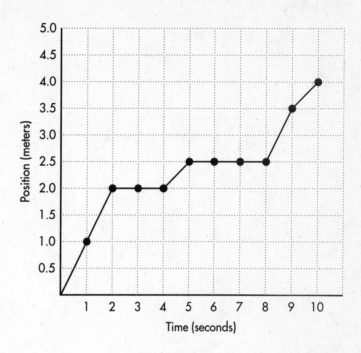

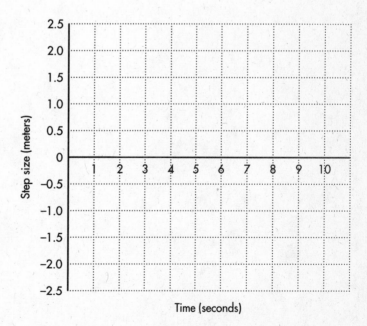

Two Kinds of Graphs (page 2 of 2)

Time (seconds)	Position	Step size

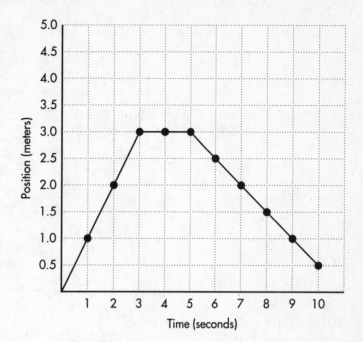

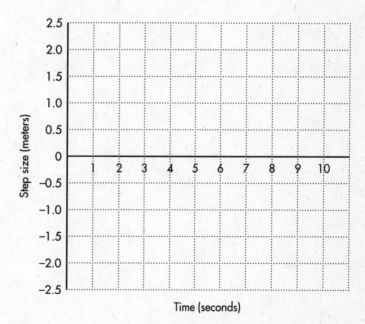

Position vs. Time Graph

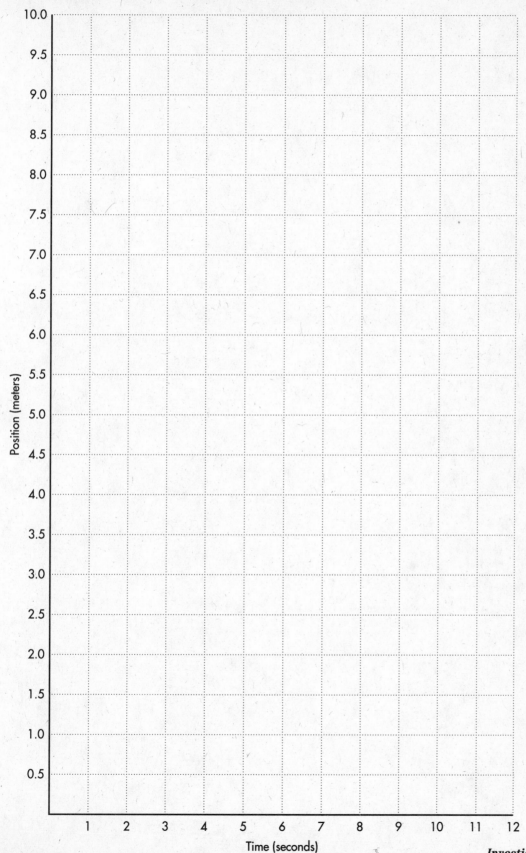

Step Size vs. Time Graph

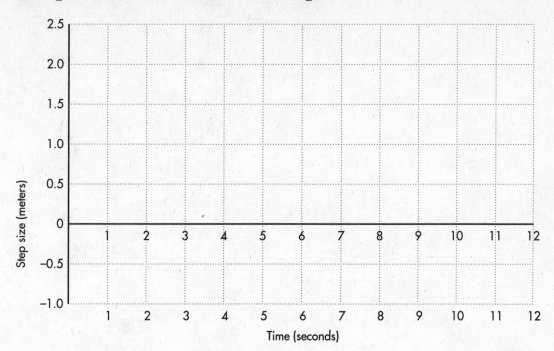

Mystery Walks (page 1 of 2)

1. She walked slowly for 3 seconds. Then she stood still for 4 seconds. Suddenly, during the last 3 seconds, she went quite fast.

2. She ran fast for 3 seconds, then slowly for 4 seconds. Then she went back to the beginning in 5 seconds.

3. He waited for 4 seconds before starting to walk slowly with a step size of 0.5. He walked for a few seconds and then stopped.

4. He walked backward very slowly. After 5 seconds he ran forward for 5 more seconds.

5. She left home running really fast with a step size of 1.5 meters. She went at that rate for 3 seconds, but then she realized that she had forgotten her book. She stopped for a couple of seconds to decide what to do. Then she decided that it would be too late anyway, so she went back home slowly.

6. From his house to the corner store is 10 meters. He ran to the store, spent 1 second looking at the CLOSED sign, and walked slowly back to his house.

7. She decided to cross the park walking slowly at first but going faster and faster each step. It took her 5 seconds to get to the other side.

8. He was going home, not in a rush. As he stepped into the street, he realized that a car was coming. He waited for the car, then ran across the street. As soon as he got to the other side of the street, he walked slowly again.

81

Mystery Walks (page 2 of 2)

9. At first the old man walked very slowly, as if he was tired. Suddenly, when he was next to us, he started to run amazingly fast. After a few seconds he stopped and walked back to say, "I surprised you, didn't I?"

10. The dog ran off to catch the stick that his owner had thrown. As the dog grabbed the stick, he saw a rabbit. The dog held very still for a moment. Then, instead of running back to his owner, he crept very slowly toward the rabbit. When the dog was close to the rabbit, he jumped forward at great speed.

11. First she went fast, at a steady pace. Then, at around 5 meters, she started to slow down. She went slower and slower until she stopped. She stood still for 4 seconds. Finally she walked slowly and steadily for a while.

12. Trying not to wake anyone up, she walked very slowly with small steps. Once she got to the door, she began to run faster and faster. After 3 seconds of running, she stopped and sat down.

13. Imagine someone walking back and forth two times between the chalkboard and her desk. She always walks fast toward the board and slowly toward the desk. At the end she remains still for 3 seconds.

14. He waited for 4 seconds before starting to run with a step size of 1.5. He ran for a few seconds and then stopped.

15. It is 8 meters between her bedroom and the kitchen. She walked into the kitchen slowly because she was half asleep, and then just stared at the room for a moment. Then she went back to bed very quickly.

What's the Story? (page 1 of 2)

Cut out these graphs. Match them with the
stories on the next page.

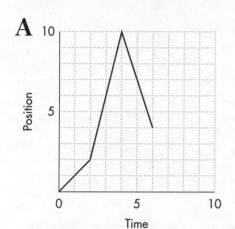

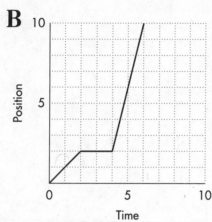

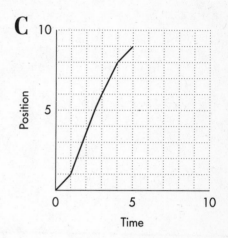

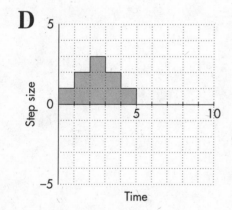

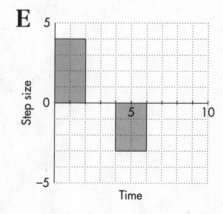

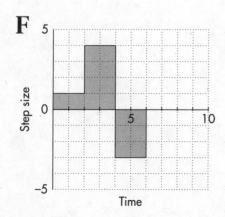

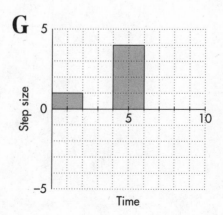

What's the Story? (page 2 of 2)

Below each story, paste the two graphs that fit the story.
Write how you know *those* graphs go with *that* story.

Story 1 I went very slowly for 2 seconds, then stopped
for 2 seconds, then went very fast to the end.

Story 2 I started slowly and went faster and faster. Then
I went slower and slower.

Story 3 I went slowly for a while and then fast to the end.
Then I turned around and came part of the way back in
the other direction.

Graphing a Motion Story

Draw a step size vs. time graph and a position vs. time graph for this motion story:

The lioness was hunting. She walked very slowly for 4 seconds. Then she stood perfectly still for 5 seconds. Suddenly, she pounced, moving very fast for 3 seconds.

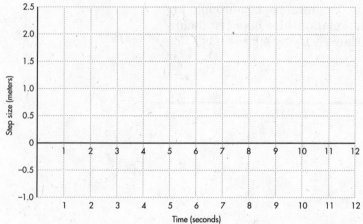

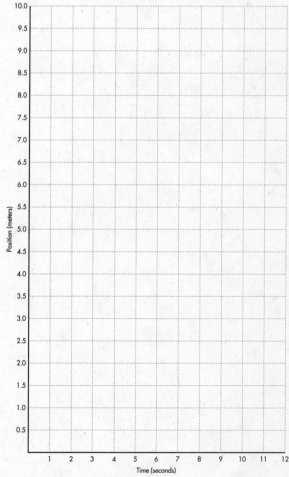

To the Family

Graphing a Motion Story

Sessions 5–6

Math Content
Making graphs of step size versus time and position versus time

Materials
Student Sheet 26
Pencil

In class, we have been exploring the relationship between graphs of position versus time and graphs of step size versus time. For homework, your child will draw one of each of these kinds of graphs to correspond to a motion story about a lioness hunting. You might ask your child to describe what each graph shows and the relationships between them, and to explain how each type of graph shows varying speeds (fast, slow, stopped).

How to Play the Digits Game

Materials: Numeral Cards (with Wild Cards removed)
Digits Game Score Sheet for each player

Players: 2 or 3

How to Play

1. Decide on the target number to use.

   Example: The target is 1000.

2. Deal the Numeral Cards. Deal out one more card than there are digits in the target.

   Example: The target has four digits, so you deal out five cards: 3, 8, 0, 1, and 5.

3. Players use the numerals on the cards to make a number as close as possible to the target.

   Example: You can use 3, 8, 0, 1, and 5 to make 1035, 853, or other numbers.

4. Write the target and the number you made on your score sheet. Find and record the difference between them.

   Example: 1000 − 853 = 147. The difference is your score.

5. When everyone has finished, compare answers. Which number is closest to the target? Is it possible to make a number even closer?

   Example: Player A made 853. Player B made 1305. Who is closer? Can you make a number with these digits that is even closer to 1000?

6. For the next round, mix up all the cards and deal a new set.

7. After three rounds, total your scores. Lowest total wins.

Digits Game Score Sheet

For each round you play, record the target number and the closest number you can make with your digits. Put the larger one first. Then find and record the difference between them.

Game 1 target: _____   Difference

Round 1: _____ – _____ = _____

Round 2: _____ – _____ = _____

Round 3: _____ – _____ = _____

Total score: _____

Game 2 target: _____   Difference

Round 1: _____ – _____ = _____

Round 2: _____ – _____ = _____

Round 3: _____ – _____ = _____

Total score: _____

Game 3 target: _____   Difference

Round 1: _____ – _____ = _____

Round 2: _____ – _____ = _____

Round 3: _____ – _____ = _____

Total score: _____

Digits Game Score Sheet

For each round you play, record the target number and the closest number you can make with your digits. Put the larger one first. Then find and record the difference between them.

Game 1 target: _____   Difference

Round 1: _____ – _____ = _____

Round 2: _____ – _____ = _____

Round 3: _____ – _____ = _____

Total score: _____

Game 2 target: _____   Difference

Round 1: _____ – _____ = _____

Round 2: _____ – _____ = _____

Round 3: _____ – _____ = _____

Total score: _____

Game 3 target: _____   Difference

Round 1: _____ – _____ = _____

Round 2: _____ – _____ = _____

Round 3: _____ – _____ = _____

Total score: _____

0	0	1	1
0	0	1	1
2	2	3	3
2	2	3	3

Practice Page
Patterns of Change

4	4	5	5
4	4	5	5
<u>6</u>	<u>6</u>	7	7
<u>6</u>	<u>6</u>	7	7

Practice Page
Patterns of Change

8	8	9	9
8	8	9	9
WILD CARD	WILD CARD		
WILD CARD	WILD CARD		

Practice Page A

Fill in the numbers you say if you start at 500 and count down by each counting number.

Count down by 25	Count down by 50	Count down by 100	Count down by 125	Count down by _____ (your choice)
500	500	500	500	500
_____	_____	_____	_____	_____
_____	_____	_____	_____	_____
_____	_____	_____	_____	_____
_____	_____	_____	_____	_____
_____	_____	_____	_____	_____
_____	_____	_____	_____	_____
_____	_____	_____	_____	_____
_____	_____	_____	_____	_____
_____	_____	_____	_____	_____
_____	_____	_____	_____	_____
_____	_____	_____	_____	_____

Practice Page B

Fill in the numbers you say if you start at 40 and count up
by each counting number.

Count up by 5	Count up by 10	Count up by 50	Count up by 250	Count up by _____ (your choice)
40	40	40	40	40
_____	_____	_____	_____	_____
_____	_____	_____	_____	_____
_____	_____	_____	_____	_____
_____	_____	_____	_____	_____
_____	_____	_____	_____	_____
_____	_____	_____	_____	_____
_____	_____	_____	_____	_____
_____	_____	_____	_____	_____
_____	_____	_____	_____	_____
_____	_____	_____	_____	_____

Practice Page C

Fill in the numbers you say if you start at 2500 and count down by each counting number.

Count down by 10	Count down by 25	Count down by 50	Count down by 250	Count down by _____ (your choice)
2500	2500	2500	2500	2500
____	____	____	____	____
____	____	____	____	____
____	____	____	____	____
____	____	____	____	____
____	____	____	____	____
____	____	____	____	____
____	____	____	____	____
____	____	____	____	____
____	____	____	____	____
____	____	____	____	____
____	____	____	____	____

Practice Page D

For each problem, show how you found your solution.

Suppose that buttons come in bags of 8.

1. If there are 14 bags of buttons in a drawer, how many buttons are there altogether?

2. If there are 20 bags of buttons in a drawer, how many buttons are there altogether?

3. If there are 34 bags of buttons in a drawer, how many buttons are there altogether?

Practice Page E

For each problem, show how you found your solution.

Suppose that sports cards come in packs of 9.

1. If one box holds 24 packs, how many sports cards are there altogether?

2. If one box holds 50 packs, how many sports cards are there altogether?

3. If one box holds 72 packs, how many sports cards are there altogether?